I0095535

AntiWar

Ron Jacobs

Copyright © 2025 Ron Jacobs

ISBN: 978-1-967022-02-1

Fomite
Burlingon, VT
fomitepress.com

It was the day before I turned ten years old. Our life on the small US Air Force base near Peshawar (West)Pakistan was fairly idyllic. When the US determined it "needed" a radar post near the Soviet Union and China, it decided that this region of Pakistan would be an excellent site. After convincing the Pakistani government that it should align itself with Washington and procuring some land in exchange for a certain amount of ongoing military and other support, the Department of Defense had done its best to recreate an American suburb in the arid lands of the subcontinent's Northwest Frontier. Two and three bedroom ramblers with carports and driveways were arranged on streets that looked like the newest Levittowns being built outside of cities around the United States. Like those suburbs, the population of the base was mostly white; one African-American family and one Puerto Rican family were the only non-white families on base. The GIs who worked at the radar installation and in various support roles lived in barracks a bit away from the family quarters. As "dependents" our interaction with these men took place mostly at the base swimming pool, which was open much of the year because of Pakistan's hot climate.

Anyhow, the date was Sunday,

September 12, 1965. My siblings and I were outdoors playing when seemingly out of nowhere a loud siren began to whine. One of my younger brothers began to cry, screaming in fright. My older sister and I did what we could to console him. Our mom told us not to worry—it was just a test of the air raid warning system. This wasn't an ordinary occurrence. There had never been any such test before since we had moved to the base in the autumn of 1963. A couple of my siblings and I were aware of the intensifying war between India and Pakistan that had begun earlier in the year. The war itself was over the mostly mountainous state called Jammu-Kashmir. This piece of land was an after thought of Britain's recently destroyed empire. After India achieved its independence in 1947—an act which was simultaneous with the bloody partition of the Indian land mass into the state of India and Pakistan—Britain had left Kashmir in a state of uncertainty. While its people mostly hoped for independence, India had other plans. So did Pakistan. A state of armed unease replaced the previous situation. The 1965 conflict was the most recent time that unease had broken out into full war.

While the US base was officially in no danger of being attacked, the fact was that the Indian Air Force wanted to destroy the airport shared by the US Air Force, the Pakistani Air Force, the CIA and civilian airlines and pilots. The men in the Pentagon, Fort Meade and Peshawar who made such decisions were putting plans in place to minimize any accidental bombings by the warring militaries. The windows of every building on base had been painted black, there was a night time curfew and blackout on the base, and Pakistanis' ability to enter the base was severely restricted. The older children knew enough from overheard conversations among adults to come up with their own speculative explanations. The younger ones could feel the uncertainty and the fear of the adults. It was an unordinary time in what seemed like rather ordinary lives.

By the time my sister and I got our brother calmed down, the all-clear siren sounded. This caused him to start crying again. After all, what did he know about all-clear or whatever? The siren was loud and it was scary. And it had never wailed before. My sister and at least one other sibling knew about air raid sirens from a couple years earlier during the nuclear showdown we call the Cuban Missile Crisis. It was at our elementary school twenty miles from Washington DC where we had first heard its threatening and menacing wail. The practice drills we were subject to in those days of November 1962 required us to sit under our school desks and pray with the nuns holding their giant rosaries while they sat under theirs. Even then, the sight of a fully-cloaked nun sitting under her desk made the more sacrilegious of us school kids snicker. Nuclear war meant nobody could maintain their dignity.

The next day was September 13, 1965. It also happened to be my tenth birthday. I celebrated with my class at the elementary school on base. After school was over my siblings and I headed home, just like any other day. After a dinner of hamburgers and frozen French fries, I blew out the candles on my birthday cake and we continued the standard family birthday celebration. Cake, ice cream, and the opening of a couple presents. By eight o'clock in the evening, I was in one of the top bunks in the bedroom I shared with my three brothers. We conversed quietly, each of us slowly drifting off to sleep. It was perhaps three hours later when I awoke, startled from my sleep by a series of loud bangs and a very loud rattling of the bedroom windows. None of my brothers woke up. Although the windows were painted black, I had scratched off the paint in the corner of the window nearest my bunk. Peeking through the transparent one inch square I could see bright flashes of light in the distance and long traces of yellowish light streaming across the sky. I realized then that what I was seeing were bomb explosions and ammunition being fired from anti-aircraft artillery. I woke up quickly, climbed from my bed and ran into my parents' room. My mother was already awake. She told me to gather my siblings and get them into the hallway. Perhaps five minutes later, our entire family of ten was squeezed into the hall of the house, half asleep or crying. My father told us we needed to start praying, so we did. Hail Marys and the Lord's Prayer over and over. We spent most of that night in the hallway. When morning came, we washed up, got dressed, and ate breakfast. My dad went to work and those of us in school went off to school.

Needless to say, school was not the regular mix of reading, writing and arithmetic. The teachers did their best to steer our conversations to the lessons they had planned, but they too had gone without much sleep and were as uncertain about what happened next as we were. Most of them were women in their twenties from around the United States. To add to their concern was that as adults they were expected to maintain a level of calm as if nothing was out of the ordinary. The rumors were flying. Some were about what had been destroyed at the airport and in downtown Peshawar. Other rumors were in regards to our future in Pakistan. Would all the women and children be shipped back to the States, leaving the men in Pakistan to defend the base? Was the Soviet Union going to join the war on India's side and if so, would the US join the Pakistani side? These were some of the questions raised in the classrooms of the older children. The questions were based on those previously mentioned overheard conversations and snippets from the base newsletter that brought us our news off the teletype located in what was mysteriously called the Operations Building. As for the younger students, many of them left with their mothers during lunch.

When school ended for the day, we walked home to discover that enlisted men had dug trenches in the backyards of many houses while we sat at our school desks. The trenches were four to five feet deep, three to four feet wide and ten to twenty feet long. Each trench was covered by sheets of heavy plywood upon which the dirt from the trenches was piled. Gaps at each end of the trench provided access. These were our air raid shelters. That night the Indian Air Force planes came again. The air raid siren sounded and families made their way into the trenches for whatever safety they might provide. We could hear the explosions from the bombs and the sounds of the Pakistani defenses—anti-aircraft weapons and other artillery. I was sitting at one end of the trench in our yard and was able to see the tracers stream across the sky. We ended up spending the entire night in the makeshift shelter. The same was true for the next four nights. On September 19, 1965, the women and children were evacuated from the air station as part of an operation the military called Nice Way. The operation itself ultimately evacuated over 1400 US civilians from East and West Pakistan during the operation, of which 372 were from Peshawar..

We had spent the day before—a Saturday—packing one bag each. Mostly, we packed clothes. My younger siblings were allowed to bring one or two toys with them; a doll, a truck or some other favorite plaything. I suppose the hope was that these items would provide them some solace in the days ahead; days filled with the unknown and varying levels of dread and fear depending on one's response to the events about to unfold. I brought a couple of science fiction paperbacks. That Saturday night was spent in the trenches once again. It would be the last one.

Sunday morning we ate breakfast and walked with our gear to the athletic field on base. A few blue schoolbuses were parked nearby. These buses were familiar to us from our class trips to downtown Peshawar and other environs off-base. Airmen helped families place their suitcases on one of the buses. We were allowed to bring a small bag with snacks, toothbrushes and things like books and toys on the bus we would be riding in. The children said goodbye to their fathers and the husbands and wives got in their hugs and kisses. Many tears were shed. After one more roll call, the Pakistani bus drivers closed the doors to the buses, revved their engines and we headed towards the Afghan-Pakistan border. Besides the women and children, there was a doctor and a couple of US military policemen on the buses. I remember the weather as being typical September weather for the region— dry, high skies and probably around eighty degrees Fahrenheit. The journey took us up into the Hindu Kush range of the Himalayas and through the Khyber Pass. The roads were narrow and winding. Most of them were paved but they were still treacherous. The Pakistani drivers were probably chosen for their knowledge of and expertise in driving on the roads.

As we rode towards the mountains I looked out the window for signs of the combat I had heard the previous few nights. I saw destroyed buildings along the roadside—mostly small buildings made from the mud and straw bricks most Pakistanis used to build their homes. I remember seeing a few dead farm animals laying in the ditches that crisscrossed the sugarcane fields, their limbs missing and carrion birds picking at their eyes and entrails. The doctor riding with us suggested that most of the damage had been at the airport since the intention of the Indian military was to destroy Pakistan's air force. He and I carried on a conversation about the war and war in general on and off during the trip to Kabul, Afghanistan—our first destination. We arrived there that night and were assigned to stay with various US Embassy personnel for the night. Our family stayed in a beautiful large home that had been built during the years of the Raj. There were large ceiling fans hanging from the high ceilings slowly moving the air. His wolfhounds were friendly and seemed to enjoy having people around willing to play with them. Our host was a senior member of the diplomatic staff with a multitude of servants. Even at the age of ten, I knew the situation was colonialist as hell. We slept and ate well. My mother, who was eight moths pregnant, said she had the best sleep of the last couple of months in the bed our host provided her.

The next morning the evacuees were taken to the Kabul airport. A couple of C-130s awaited us. C-130s were the largest cargo planes operated by the US military at the time. Although they were mostly used to transport various cargoes, sometimes they were outfitted with a type of strapping that served as seats so that troops could be moved from base to base. That was the scenario we encountered as we entered the planes. To say the least, this arrangement was not particularly comfortable. Before takeoff, the doctor distributed motion-sickness pills to everyone. I did not take mine. While I watched my fellow evacuees drift off to sleep I read comics and one of the books I had brought along. Eventually, one of the crewmen came back to check on the passengers. Seeing I was awake, he asked if I wanted to join him in the cockpit. Naturally, I jumped at the chance.

After a refueling stop in Tehran, Iran—which was ruled at the time by one of Washington's favorite dictators, Shah Reza Pahlavi—we headed to Istanbul, Turkey. While we were in Tehran, Red Cross workers gave each of us a bag lunch. Mine contained a couple baloney and lettuce sandwiches, an apple and some cookies. The children also received a stack of comic books if they wanted them. I took a couple. My mother was provided a bit of a respite from her burden when a couple of the Red Cross workers entertained and fed her youngest children. We got back on the plane fed and ready for the last leg of the flight. After landing in Istanbul, we once again boarded buses. These buses took us to our final destination for the time being, Karamursel Air Station. This imperial outpost lay across the Straits of Marmara and was but one of many such outposts in Turkey. Once we arrived in Karamursel, we were sent to live in barracks only recently abandoned by enlisted men who had been reassigned to tents and other temporary quarters.

Although we were moved around inside the buildings, we stayed in those barracks for three months while the Indian and Pakistani governments negotiated a truce. At the superpower level, Moscow and Washington agreed to stop supplying arms and ammunition to the warring states. As the supply of arms dwindled the truce talks became more serious. The Indian and Pakistanis militaries were quickly discovering that it was pretty much impossible to fight a war without a resupply of the lethal materials armed conflict demands. In the 1960s, the nature of the arms industry made it almost impossible for smaller militaries to obtain large shipments of arms from somewhere else if Washington or Moscow stopped sending their provisions.

In short, the war ended because the weapons supplies stopped.

As I write this, the news is reporting that the US government is sending an "emergency" shipment of weapons to Israel. The estimated dollar value of this shipment is three billion dollars. According to CBS News, it includes 35,500 MK 84 and BLU-117 bombs and 4,000 Predator warheads worth $2.04 billion. (3/1/2025) This shipment is a continuation of Washington's decades-long arming of Israel and its ongoing, illegal and brutal siege and occupation of Palestine. The Congress has another twelve billion dollars of mostly military aid for Israel on its agenda. On another front, the current president of Ukraine is continuing his years-long tour dedicated to procuring weapons and financial support for the Ukrainian military's role in the imperial rivalry between Washington and Moscow. Although the reasons for this armed conflict are still being debated and seemingly dependent on whether one thinks Russia is more despicable than Washington or the opposite, the fact that the trumpist White House suspended arms supplies shipments to Kyiv verifies my earlier statement. That is that it's "pretty much impossible to fight a war without a resupply of the lethal materials armed conflict demands." Since Washington has suspended its shipments (at least temporarily), Kyiv's choices seem to be to negotiate a truce and peace agreement or hustle some weapons from another set of suppliers. Unfortunately, today's global arms industry involves manufacturers and financiers in multiple countries, not to mention those suppliers in the unregulated arms markets. This means that Kyiv and other governments intent on war can turn to other suppliers should the US refuse to supply them. Add to this dynamic the fact that recent history seems to indicate that Washington would rather supply weapons to its clients and neocolonies than insist that they negotiate seriously. More honestly, the fact that the war industry is such a crucial part of the US economy is what induces Washington to reject any meaningful peace talks for as long as it can.

Back to my story about Pakistan. Why did I open this essay with it? What is my point? Briefly stated, I wrote it to provide an example of the many unseen consequences of war. What begins as words between ruling classes turns into wars between armies. These wars uproot, maim and kill civilians and soldiers alike without discrimination. While the experience of my family and the rest of the US residents of that base in Peshawar was disruptive and even scary, it pales substantially in relation to the experience of the Pakistani families whose homes were bombed, their livelihoods upended or destroyed and their family members killed or wounded. The trauma of my experience most likely played a role in my future, but its negative effects still seem minimal. Indeed, I believe that the US war on Vietnam affected me more negatively than anything else in my life, even though I was never in the military or in Vietnam. I did participate in the movement against that war though and my father spent over a year in DaNang later in the decade. Coincidentally, the fall of 1965 was also when the United States removed all of the women and children stationed there with US forces from southern Vietnam as that war spiraled towards disaster. On the other hand, other base residents involved in the same situation in Peshawar suffered from PTSD which manifested itself both then and later.

When I think of war today in Palestine, Ukraine, and elsewhere, I can't help but think of the effects my brush with war had on my family and friends in Peshawar. When I see video of children being peppered with automatic weapons fire and adolescents burned alive in Gaza, I can not even imagine the pain suffered, both physical and emotional. When I watch hospitals being bombarded, homes being set afire, and aid trucks destroyed by the Israeli military I realize there is not enough experience in my being to understand or even wholly imagine what the targets of that military feel. When I read of Russian and Ukrainian counterattacks on energy infrastructure in the cold northern winter, I ask myself how can these politicians, generals and profiteers be so uncaring? On both sides, the people whose lives they are upending are the same people they claim they are fighting for.

To know that both conflicts could be steered towards peace, towards a truce, if the weapons stopped flowing makes the suffering I see from afar even less acceptable, even more unexplainable. The next statement is not written to deny the responsibility of Ukraine and Israel's adversaries. However, it is intended to force the reader to consider (or reconsider, as the case may be), the primary role the United States government and the arms industry it works for in the world's armed conflicts.

If the United States wanted a fair-handed peace in the world, it could lead the way in proceeding to that goal. Instead, it continues to insist on its drive toward world hegemony and domination. This is in large part because of the capitalist economy and its need to expand and extract, consume and control. Any honest observer of the last one hundred fifty years would have to admit this essential truth. Furthermore, their honesty would demand the acknowledge-ment that US capitalism's current modus operandi is more avaricious than ever before in history. It is that same history which indicates that the destruction of the environment, the growing number of the poor, and the continuing atomization and isolation in the human community will only get worse ever more quickly as long as capitalism remains on the trajectory it is on. I would further argue that wars will continue until capitalism itself is gone.

As I mentioned earlier, one other element in the current stage of capitalism is the import-ance of the war industry. Rosa Luxemburg put it this way in her 1915 Junius Pamphlet: "The high stage of world-industrial development in capitalistic production finds expression in the extraordinary technical development and destructiveness of the instruments of war." This in itself explains a lot about why war is the go-to response to disagreements involving the United States, its vassals and its outposts. Although the Pentagon is often hesitant to commit large numbers of US forces to most conflicts, the US war machine shows little hesitation about committing other nations' troops to armed conflict. Perhaps the most glaring example of this today is Washington's role in the preparation for war and the continuation of war in Ukraine.

So wait, you might say. Am I calling for an end to arms shipments to Israel and Ukraine? How can I compare the two conflicts? Maybe it's clear that Israel will only stop its murderous attempt to destroy the very idea of Palestine is to stop sending it weapons, but how can someone support cutting of weapons to Kyiv? Let me quote a piece I wrote for Counterpunch in February 2024.

When the tools of war are depleted or denied, the participants in said conflict have to seek some other means to end it. Total victory for either side becomes an illusion impossible to attain, even in their own dreams. Lives are saved. The political and economic interests that propelled the armies to wage war must seek other means of conflict resolution. In other words, they must sit down and negotiate a ceasefire, maybe even a permanent truce. In the conflicts in Palestine and Ukraine, it is well past time for the United States and its subsidiaries to stop deliveries of weapons and ammunition. No participant in either conflict can win militarily, no matter what the...leaders involved think or say. The roots of the conflicts are political, as are the means to resolve them. I repeat, Washington, as the primary arms merchant in both conflicts, must end its shipments immediately. Only then will the political actors involved begin to talk. Only then will the way towards a fair and reasonable peace open up....

.... In Palestine, the people and their resistance groups will have an opportunity to take care of their immediate survival. In Ukraine, where both Moscow and Kyiv have alternately called for negotiations instead of war, a similar scenario would unfold. Maintaining and supporting a military approach places territory and power above human life and, at its most fundamental puts war industry profits above peace. In doing so, the continued dominance of the masters of war is guaranteed. And the unnecessary loss of life goes on."

The time to stop the war machine is way past due. Previous attempts like the so-called peace dividend in the 1990s ended before they started. Despite his talk of being against war, Donald Trump's words will be tested if he actually tries to stifle the US war machine. Already, the Musk-Trump blitzkrieg attack on the US budget has largely left the Pentagon budget alone except for the removal of so-called woke texts and monuments honoring Black and female soldiers and the termination of various offices focused on fighting racism, sexism and heterosexism in the military and its recruiting process. The business of war and preparing for war is too profitable to let it go. Indeed, Musk and his empire makes much of its money in the business of war. Not even Trump's uncanny ability to convince voters, business-people and politicians to go along with his program will override the war industry's power.

War will not end as long as people accept it as reasonable. People will continue to accept it as reasonable as long as peace negotiations are ridiculed, considered impossible or ignored by at least one of the adversaries. War's long history among humans does not explain it away nor justify its continued existence. The intensification of war's bloodshed and devastation since the advent of capitalism and industrialization has only made the necessity for war to end more important. The fact that it hasn't ended strengthens the argument that it is not the majority of humanity that decides to go to war, but those with the power and the money that makes those decisions. *Wars against colonialism and imperialism would not occur if both of those phenomena—phenomena inextricably linked to capitalism—ceased to exist. Likewise, wars between capitalist nations—wars which carry a great potential to become world wars—would also become a thing of the past.*

Any movement to end today's wars and work towards preventing tomorrow's must begin with this understanding. Short of that, even the task of ending today's wars becomes that much more difficult.

Yet, we must persevere.

www.ingramcontent.com/pod-product-compliance
Lightning Source LLC
Chambersburg PA
CBHW032104020426
42335CB00011B/490